DIVA

Short Sale

A Self Proclaimed Short Sale DIVA's
Guide to Surviving Short Sales

Joey McCune Moore

Dear Reluctant Realtor,

(Although i suppose some know-it-all's are peeking and their must be some out there who have mastered it as I have (but you didn't' write a book NOW did you?)--- the majority of you, however, are reluctant and wondering what the hell you are getting into. This ~~bud's~~ i mean, book's for YOU).

Welcome to my book.

I am a book lover. When i am interested in a book, I tend to read the first paragraph to see if i like the feel or tone of it. If you are reading this, i can only assume that you're thinking twice.

Maybe you're thinking *"i don't know much about Short Sales (..Hmmm...) i would like more information. I hear they are horrible and i should stay away!?" Or maybe you are asking yourself, "should i buy a book based solely on the ever-so-appealing cover?"* **Well, that's a good enough reason for me.**

Do i really need to add that there are secret tidbits for "short sale success" you will only learn after the book is purchased? **"HELLO",** *everyone* **can use a tidbit for success!**--- Why are you STILL reading?

Look, your wishy-washy attitude is really starting to bug me. You know what? Maybe you should put the freaking book down and let someone who might want to *make some money*, buy it! I'm sorry. That was uncalled for. #Deep breath... #finding self-control. I'm sure in some circles you're considered successful? I'm sure by now you're skipping past that register... What! You're STILL not buying it? What's the matter, you can't read? Who cares? **I can't write.**

All right, FINE, you win. **YOU WIN!**
I'll tell you a little about the book.

The first thing you should know is: **I dig short sales.**

Here are some of the helpful suggestions you'll get by reading this book:

1) It's always a good idea to live life with humor. Without a little humor, none of us would survive the rollercoaster ride of negotiating a short sale.
2) If you aren't naturally organized, then you better hire someone who is...
3) Have a large supply of your favorite headache medicine i.e.: advil, tylenol, vicadin... for those days when you think you're getting a paycheck ...and then you don't.
4) Make sure you have a good stream of friends, family and the like to complain to when you need to vent (they will need to be good friends, because they will get sick of it pretty quickly)
5) Grow a pair. Balls, that is. It takes balls to negotiate a successful transaction, dealing with both the Sellers (in crisis), and the Banks ($8 an hour) loss mitigators. Prepare. Drink milk. Do whatever you have to do.

Convinced? I thought so. Just remember: sometimes you *can* judge a book by its cover, or in this case, its tremendously well designed cover.

You hold in your hands the most unique and entertaining guide to short sales ever written (although i AM my BIGGEST fan).

A no-nonsense, tough-love guide for savvy realtors who want to start making some money and get their short sale swagger on.

I'll see you on the inside.

The DIVA

Dedicated to...

My adoring and HUNKY husband--- **Mitch**, who puts me on the pedestal i so love and appreciate. My two fantastic ROCK STAR teenagers who are *made out of awesome* --**Emma and Jackson**, and my always sidekick, furry assistant, **Bentley**.

But, MOSTLY to Bentley, since he knows the inside scoop, is there day-in and day-out, never calls in sick, is an absolute vault when it comes to client privacy, and always forgives me after witnessing a swearing tangent.

Joey McCune Moore

Your heard me correctly. That's Joey, J-o-e-y like a boy, but i'm a girl. (Yes, i am a woman #hear me roar). Joey is a woman's name too! I get asked all the time if my

parents wanted a boy. NO, they did NOT. WANT.A.BOY. I am named after Joey Heatherton, a totally HAWT sex kitten, actress, singer, and chick from the 60's. And really, people-- I would be a pretty fem dude if i was a guy with a DIVA crown on my cover. Not that it's not possible--- i have plenty of DIVA guy friends, especially in Real Estate. That's why it's pink. I LOVE pink. Pink is my favorite color, because it's a pretty "girly" color, but also because i am a girly girl. Not at all a tomboy type. Well, a little bit of a tomboy type, but I'm trying to make a point here. Don't give me shit about my name. It's annoying.

Master Bentley, posing for his debut

TABLE OF *all important* CONTENTS

CHAPTER 1:

Gym Terminology

In MY gym (#Cross Fit RULES), when things get tough, a popular saying is often overheard, **"GET SOME".**

In my opinion, Gym terminology can be quite fitting for short sale negotiations.

First of all---
~~In the gym~~ (**at the office**) You have to be ~~athletic minded~~ (**competitive minded**)—and feed on the excitement of ~~competition~~ (**negotiation**). In the end, we all like to win, none of us like to lose, and it's a ~~good sport~~ (**seasoned agent**) that knows how to ~~play the game~~ (**successfully negotiate and close a short sale transaction**).

*That's all i really had to say about that. I thought it was pretty good though. Apply that to your mindset. # **Get SOME!***

CHAPTER 2:

Short Sales - The Modern Day Back-Alley Abortion

Now,

Whether you live in a trailer with the income of a 13 year old girl, or on an award-winning vineyard in Napa, the plethora of short sales, their rapid growth and expected upward trend is a freak show reality that has surely affected you, one of your neighbors, your town, city, and definitely your state. If we are going to sell real estate, anywhere, we have to deal with them. Knowing how to deal with them is giving a gift to yourself. It's the giving of yourself *(because believe me Honey, you're gonna be tired)*, a present of you *(your made out of awesomeness)*, to them *(your clients)*, from me *(my already pointed out awesomeness)*, for us *(our awesomeness together)*. Everybody is a winner.

The truth is, *Sweetheart*, If you haven't lost 30-60% of your assets in the last few years, then you didn't have any assets. Am I right, or am i right? We're all feeling the pain. And it hurts. Realtors are certainly no exception.

Yes, we still see the occasional listing that's not a short sale or REO and the fact is, either Grandma lives there or a Jew – 'cause everyone else and their brother took out a home equity line of credit and bought a flat screen, a Range Rover, or a boat, are in deep, and are either under on their mortgage or still doing their very best to hold on. You and i both know those are not the typical phone calls we are receiving for listings.

This book will hopefully help you not shudder and break into a cold sweat when you hear the dreaded term "short sale". The term that most agents are hiding from because they either:

A) don't understand them,
B) are too lazy to deal with them,
C) haven't realized what a gold mine they are, or
D) are spawn from the wrong end of the gene pool and are too stupid anyway. These weaklings should simply hire agents like me to make all the money and throw a referral fee back their way.

No, seriously (about D).

But really, … **YOU CAN DO IT**. It's not that hard.
Jesus, if i can, anyone can. And i rock. #just sayin'.
This witty little book is my attempt to share with you something i take very seriously; negotiating short sales, my way, my style. I have grown so FREAKING tired of dealing with agents that *think* they understand short sales, and *screw the whole damn deal up.* **IT'S JUST NOT THAT HARD, PEOPLE!**

SOoo, really this is my way of trying to help save the world, one short sale at a time. Just in case i have the buyer and you are the negotiator and just in case you are the buyer and one of my books taught some idiot agent how to **GET SOME.**

It may not be the proper way, or the most traditional, ~~or even legal~~ (just kidding) way, but it works for me. I can't write well, but i can negotiate the H-E – double LL out of a short sale even better, and i am willing to share my process, that because of its proven success, i continue to make **$** (money), over and over again **$$$$** (Lots of Money!) And isn't that what this is really all about? #Hell ya it is.

With the downfall of the economy and the real estate bubble officially popped, Short sales are an ever-growing trend. Sellers are embarrassed and don't want to admit their failure, Agents don't want to talk about them too often in case their buyers want to focus on them. It's a true "hush-hush" term that tends to send off a vibe of "do not enter" or "NEXT" (when touring clients), but to little ole' me it is a charmingly old-fashioned term reminiscent of the "back alley abortion". This shit is happening whether we like it or not. And there's a chunk of money to be made!

Don't get me wrong, I like the old school way of listing a house, (OH GOD HOW I MISS IT), back when we had equity, non-stressed out Sellers and bidding wars the first day we hit the market. Believe me, as a luxury home specialist, $1.0M and up until 2007, I am right along beside you wishing to turn back the clock. But as the economy has dipped, along with the $'s in my pocket book (and its pretty safe to assume yours too), i had to find a new way to pay the bills. Because when you are bringing in **$** and the Bills are **$$$$$** short sales are an awesome way to hone your skills, keep your clients happy, really help out a seller who is underwater as well as a buyer who wants a great deal, and pay those bastard bills at the same time. *I look at it this way: If i help a distressed homeowner out now, in two years, when they are back on their feet and able to buy another home, who are they going to remember? **ME**. That's right--- me. I helped them out when they needed it most. And i just betcha--- i will have some serious client satisfaction and loyalty. #case in point.*

This is not a joke book. Although, it may appear to be—but seriously-- i AM serious about all of this. This book is full of real information. Most of the little i know, i learned through trial and error, as well as Girl Scouts, and having been Prom Royalty, waking up at a frat house without my bra, some bartending school, sitcoms, listening to the radio, watching YouTube, a few webinars, oh, and did i mention, starving to death when the market crashed and throwing myself into the unknown? I was also fascinated by the constant rising foreclosure news the increasing rate of Distressed Homes, and the reality TV shows ~~with DORK realtors~~ proving real estate can still be fruitful.   *I really just want my own reality show—and now here's my chance*. Hopefully, with the help of my book, it will be your chance too.

CHAPTER 3:

All Right Already---Let's Get This Party Started!

IDENTIFYING THE PROSPECTIVE SHORT SALE SELLER.
I don't have a lot of time as i am busy negotiating multiple short sales and writing funny books. SOoo when I get a call from a prospective Seller who wants to list their home I have a format i go through to help me identify if the Seller is indeed a candidate for my time.

#bare with me, i may have newbie realtors who buy this book... so i've included the basics

My form is similar to the one below that I keep as a pdf and forward it to my prospective client prior to meeting them. This information helps me get a clear picture of what i am dealing with ahead of time. Of course, once you begin to close transactions a plethora of referrals follow and you will know ahead of time that they are a distressed property owner and you can get right to the point.

Name: _____

Property Address: _____

Mailing Adress:_____

Email:_____

Home Phone:_____

Cell Phone:_____

Work Phone:_____

Bedrooms:_____

Bathrooms:_____

Garage:_____

Pool:_____

Square Feet:_____

Why are you selling?:_____
_____

What are your plans alter the property sells? Leaving the area, or staying? Buying, or renting something else? Can i refer you to a realtor in that area?_____
_____
_____

How long have you owned this house?_____

Do you own other properties? Do you need to sell them?_____
_____

Have you made any improvements in the past few years like updating the kitchen, baths? Could you tell me a little about your house?_____
_____
_____

What are you plans if the house doesn't sell?_____
_____

When are you hoping to move by? Before/alter school? Christmas? Has your family moved already?
_____

What are houses selling for in your neighborhood? Area? Building?
_____

What price do you have in mind for your house?_____
_____

Do you have any relocation/corporate Packaged? (if yes)
Do you have a buyout?_____

Are you interviewing other realtors? Who?_____
Is your house currently on the market?_____
When do you want to put your house on the market?_____
When are you and your spouse available to meet together?_____
_____

Oh, by the way, what caused you to call me?_____
_____

Additional Notes:
What type of work do you do?_____
_____

Did you sign an employee handbook?_____
_____

Do you have any security clearances?_____
Are you bonded?_____
Does your employer know you are in foreclosure? (it may affect
your employment)_____
_____

Have you tried a loan modification?_____
How many payments are you behind? Be honest._____
Have you been served with foreclosure? Did you respond?_____
Do you understand how a short sale is much better than a
foreclosure?_____
Are you considering bankruptcy?_____
Have you spoken with anyone else about your house / foreclosure /
short sale? Who? _____
_____

What is your hardship in a nutshell? _____
_____
_____
_____

Is your spouse or other people on the deed/mortgage on board with a short sale? _____
_____

Do you or anyone still live in the house? Is it rented? Do they know what is going on?_____

Is there anything else that i should know about your situation? Please be honest: _____
_____
_____
_____

Do you have computer and printer access?_____
_____

Do you know other people in this situation? How can i help them?_____
_____

CHAPTER 4:

Mortgaged To The Freaking Hilt

After identifying that they are either distressed, mortgaged to the *#$% ing hilt, have lost a job, simply cannot sell their house for what it is worth, or all of the above, this is what I do:

I like to obtain as much information as possible when i meet with a prospective seller, always, but especially when they are a short sale. **I ask a lot of questions to identify how serious the seller is, and what type of hardship you are looking to deal with** as well as if their Jobs will be jeopardized (in the off chance you are unable to obtain short sale approval and the house goes into active foreclosure, some types of Jobs can be affected), and exactly how **motivated** the seller is. It is VERY IMPORTANT to identify how motivated the seller is. The seller needs to be involved for a successful transaction.

THE MEETING. Part 1:

It always sorta cracks me up when i meet with a distressed home-owner. I already know before i walk in the door that the seller is stressed financially and emotionally, their life is overwhelming and they aren't sure they can trust me with the truth about how they put themselves in this situation #or not.
It's the typical...

HO: **Hi, it's nice to meet you?** ME: **It's nice to meet you also.** (*It's not nice to meet me at all! You are embarrassed, turning red, getting anxious, about to cry and trying to hold it all together. STOP that! You're making ME feel like shit!*)

HO: **I am so sorry the house is a mess...** ME: **Please don't worry. A short sale is much different than a traditional sale and those things are much less important.** (*they all are, honey—don't you worry about it. You're in a freaking financial mess, what did you think i was expecting? This is what i see day in, day out. Glad to see the fridge is still here in this one.*)

Or,
HO: **Would you like to tour the house?** ME: **Absolutely, but later... let's talk first.**
(*NO, I DON'T NEED TO SEE YOUR FREAKING HOUSE RIGHT NOW— THE DAMN THING IS UNDERWATER, YOU CAN'T SELL IT FOR WHAT YOU OWE, YOUR HUSBAND KICKED A HOLE IN THE WALL, THE KIDS ARE STARING AT ME LIKE I AM GOING TO RUIN THEIR LIFE, AND I NEED THE HOUSE TO LOOK LIKE POOP ANYWAY!* (by the way, i hope you understand that when i type in caps, i am YELLING in my loud voice. I am Italian. I am loud. It's just me, making a point. *Now you know that i am even funnier than you thought i was*).

But my absolute favorite is: (and it happens <u>EVERY</u> time)

HO: I think we should mention that *we haven't been paying our mortgage in several months* and we want to be upfront with you. (the homeowner breaks into a low, whispers, and looks around with caution when they talk about missing payments or about anything to do with "short sales".)

ME ~~laughing~~ thinking: <u>HELLO! NO ONE CAN HEAR YOU!</u> The banks are not in the room!!! Your neighbors are not HERE!

*It just cracks me up. The whole *whispering* thing. It's the guilt. The guilt makes them *whisper.*

THE MEETING. Part 2: (for real)

Once i meet with the Sellers i explain the short sale process in entirety.
It really isn't as complicated as most people think.

I request general client information to help determine the seriousness of the situation.
I do a CMA on the home and list it to sell hopefully within 30 days of list date. A fast sale on a home is better for the clients credit if they are behind on payments and if a house is priced well enough, yes even in this market, it will get competing offers. My goal is to have at least 3 offers (an offer and 2 back ups on each listing). One thing i have learned is that buyers are impatient and even though i do my best to educate all involved, (the Sellers, the selling office agent, and the buyers) that short sales are timely, i often lose my first couple of buyers and end up with my second or third back up offer by the time the transaction closes.

I pull title to make sure there are no liens that the Sellers have "forgotten". I take into consideration all issues with the house or condo.

Sometimes there are pending assessments i have to take into consideration, sometimes back HOA's, and back taxes. All of these add up to a loss for the bank and a lesser net from your sales price. I like to try and figure out how the bank is looking at it as well.

SOME SERIOUS GOOD STUFF HERE—SO LISTEN UP...
I take the **Sold** comps and sometimes the **Pending** comps and average them individually.
If 3 houses have sold for $380K, $279K and $335K the average Solds is $330K.
I take that average and look at currently **Active** comps to compare and see if my listing will be a palpable offer for the bank. (Of course if there are 10 Solds, that is even better. I am using the number 3 for an example only. Don't be so uptight and literal. You want as many solds as possible to paint the most realistic picture).

In the above example, i would list mine at $320K, depending on days on market time that the solds and pendings and current actives have. That market time depicts whether the prices are accurate or if they are too high.

Based on that information i choose my sales price. Remember, i want my listing to sell quickly (within 30 days) so i can A) alleviate my seller's stress, B) get busy negotiating and C) so there is less deficiency to negotiate.

I discuss the listing price and CMA—showing the seller where i am coming from and why i relieve the sales price should be effective where i have placed it, backing it up with stats, and comps and *yada yada yada.*

What an Agent needs to know in a nutshell (more detail later)
EXPLAINING THE SHORT SALE PROCESS AND WHAT TO EXPECT TO THE SELLER:

- List the home / No sign / No flyers
- Targeting a buyer within 30 days, hopefully 2 or 3 buyers (that go into back up position)
- Once an offer is in mutual i put together the entire short sale packet and forward to all of the lien holders (First, Second, Third--- each one is separately negotiated).
- Remove lockbox from door
- Drop price in MLS to at or just above offer price
- Once the short sale is received and uploaded into the Banks loss mitigation system it generally takes about 2 weeks for a BPO (brokers price opinion) or an appraisal to be ordered.
- The appraiser or the BPO agent will call you to view the home. Do your best to be there and control the outcome to the best of your ability
- Once the bank has the returned appraisal/BPO on the home (usually about 10 days) a negotiator is assigned.
- Time frame is generally, but not always about 3 weeks from this point to obtain approval. If there is more than one lien, you need to handle them both separately. The second will generally need the approval from the first lien holder to move forward.
- A short sale takes "on average" about 3 months. I have seen them go much longer and i have closed some in 10 days. Each bank varies.

Always explain that a short sale is not 100% guaranteed solution. A bank may choose to not approve the short sale.

Short Sale Outcomes:
1) The bank will accept the short sale offer and release the seller from the deficiency amount in full
2) The bank can counter back with a purchase price to the buyer

3) The bank can counter back with a settlement amount the seller will need to pay

4) The bank can counter back with a promissory note, to be paid over time. Interest is usually 0% and there is usually not a pre-payment penalty. All of this can be negotiated.

5) The seller can choose to not short sale the property, which is why it is imperative that these options be explained up front, so that you do not work all the way to the end and the seller decides to not short sale or file BK. If the seller decides to file bankruptcy, you're screwed! Bankruptcy stops the entire process. Hence all the questions upfront. A short sale can move forward post BK, but usually takes at a minimum 90 days, generally 120 before you can begin again. So, if the Sellers are considering BK, make sure you let them file first and complete their Bankruptcy prior to listing the house. *One time my Sellers filed a week prior to closing (i had negotiated two approvals) and we lost our buyer, our approvals and it was pretty much a pisser.

<u>The above is why it is important to know that your listing price and offer are within about 85% - 90% of market value.</u> I have personally not seen Banks take lower offers than that. * In the above example listing (prior) it would have been listed for $320K. The average market value was $330K. 90% of $330K is $297K and 85% of $330K is $280K. I would not take an offer lower than $280K to be safe. The range i would have given the Sellers is $280K-$320K. Pricing is VERY important. Of course, if my listing was a condo with $80K worth of assessments with a pending lawsuit, and i had a miraculous cash buyer, then i would take that into consideration on price and use that as additional hardship as argument to the bank.

CHAPTER 5:

I'm Gonna Walk! #Blah. Blah. Blah.

THIS BRINGS ME TO INTRODUCE SOME IMPORTANT DIFFERENCES:

The decision to do a short sale or walk away from a home is not an easy on for a seller. And **it is an emotional decision.** Sellers will ask you why they should short sale when they could just walk away from everything. I urge you as a professional to keep up on the changes and do your research so you can best define the differences and compare them for your Sellers. Your Sellers are coming to you for assistance. They are distressed, in need of professional assistance and guidance and are often times fragile emotionally. In addition, I have excellent Real Estate Lawyers and Real Estate Accountants that i refer to all of my clients. There are many questions that are best answered by those who specialize in those fields. It is best for Sellers to first look into all of their options before they make the decision to stop paying or walk away from their mortgage. Often times, when i am called for a listing, the Sellers have not been paying their mortgage for months and sometimes over a year.

Sometimes they are in active foreclosure and have a sale date. But once in a while they have not yet missed any payments. It is NEVER legal for a real estate agent to advise a seller to not make any payments. *on that note i will mention that some Banks will flat out tell Sellers that they will not help them until they are behind. But that is not license to EVER advise anyone to go delinquent. That is illegal.

What i do know, and what may change after this book is published, Sellers will not be liable for any income taxes since the passage of the 2007 Mortgage Relief Tax law but this will expire in 2012. So any short sales or foreclosures after 2012, might end up having tax consequences. In other words, YES Sellers might end up owing income taxes of any debt forgiven in relation to a short sale or fore-closure after 2012. Even if this law didn't exist, if Sellers choose short sale over a foreclosure--they still end up ahead because their tax liability will be less on a short sale than on a foreclosure *for transactions closing after 2012.

A foreclosure is something you **DO NOT** want on your credit report. It will stay on your record for 10 years while a short sale will stay on your credit record for 5-7 years. With a short sale, you can buy a home after 2 years. With a foreclosure, you might have to wait 5-7 years, to buy again. By then, mortgage interest rates and home prices might increase to a point where one might be priced out of the market.

Foreclosure has a bigger stigma than a short sale. A foreclosure shows that you don't care about the lender's position and a short sale shows that you are a responsible person and care about miti-gating the lender's position.
Sellers get pissy and throw little bitch fits and "Why should this matter to a seller"? "Why should they care about lessening the losses for their lender"?

They will be whining that the Banks didn't care about them when they loaned money on an interest only arm! *Well—the Seller didn't care when they were taking out $50K for their new Mercedes convertible either.... It goes both ways. But you can't really say that, it makes them mad and you might not get the listing.*

Unfortunately, Foreclosure and Bankruptcy WILL matter to anyone who wants to do business with them or even to any future employers. It affects insurance premiums and interest rates on purchases.

I don't know why that is, but IT is what IT is. I don't like it as much as the next person. I didn't write the rules, I'm just informing you of them so that you are better informed about the decision to do a short sale or walk away. Obviously we are PRO Short Sale because we make money, but it's clearly a better option for a homeowner verses allowing the home to go into foreclosure, or filing bankruptcy.

Of course, every loan is different and Sellers may not have the option to do a short sale but most lenders are open to short sale as it is a better option for them verses a foreclosure or even deed in lieu. Please note that each states real estate laws are different. Please do your research on your state for short sales and distressed properties.

Contrary to what you may have heard, lenders actually want to avoid foreclosure wherever possible. That's why they're accepting more short sale and transactions everyday in an effort to eliminate unnecessary foreclosures. It won't feel like that sometimes while you are negotiating, but it is the case. This is great news for homeowners facing financial distress. And, this is GREAT NEWS for us as Realtors, who have GOT.IT.DOWN.

CHAPTER 6:

Home Owners Are Going To Drill The Hell Out Of You.

This is when i send them to my favorite Real Estate Lawyer or Real Estate Accountant. But—i also have solid knowledge about basic terminology and <u>you should too</u>. If you are hesitant and concerned you don't understand, consider what it feels like to be a homeowner in this situation! It's all CHINESE sounding to them. (Unless, of course, they are Chinese. Then it's Greek.... unless of course they are Greek... well--- you get my drift).
Here's my detail I told you was coming.

WHAT AGENTS *NEED* TO KNOW:
Every homeowner who is looking to short sale their property **will** be asking the following question: "On a short sale, will I have to pay the bank the difference between what I owe and the final sales price of my property?" The answer to this is **both yes and no**. Don't worry, I'm gonna make this simple for you to understand.

DEFINING TERMS:

Foreclosure Deficiency Judgment: A deficiency judgment is a lien against the borrower whose **foreclosure** does not produce sufficient funds to pay the mortgage in full. It is an actual judgment, that is, you are being sued. Thus, the borrower is liable to pay the difference between what they owe and what it sells for on a short sale or in an auction. The option to pursue the borrower is only available if the lender proceeds with a **Judicial Foreclosure (basically, the lender sues you for the difference)**. Keep in mind that in a **Non-Judicial Foreclosure**, the junior lien holder can **still pursue a deficiency judgment** in many states. All of this can be determined based on original loan documents and/or the type of loan/lender.

Short Sale Deficiencies as Unsecured Notes: Short sale deficiencies are realized when the **short sale** does not produce sufficient funds to pay the mortgage in full. Short sale deficiencies are typically:

- Waived in exchange for a pay off
- Accounted for via promissory note for the deficient balance or percentage of the balance
- Collected after the short sale as unsecured notes, that is, they will not be able to secure the lien against your other assets (since you've already sold the collateral property in a short sale) unless they actually sue you. Again, unless the lender/PMI/collections agency sues you in court and actually files a "deficiency judgment" against you, the note shall remain unsecured. For the most part, lenders will not sue their borrowers as it is more costly for them to do so then to keep in unsecured. Lenders often "reserve the right to pursue the deficiency" in a short sale, but what typically ends up happening is that the **unsecured note most likely ends up being substituted with a 1099 (tax on sale) for the deficient balance (which they will charge off), which most homeowners**

are exempt from (Mortgage Forgiveness Debt Relief Act of 2007).
*until 2012.

*Google the shit out of this stuff if you don't understand it. Call a Real Estate Lawyer
and a Real Estate Accountant and ask them questions. Its 10 minutes of your time
and the first hand knowledge will serve you well*

Invoice for the Deficiency/ Sued for a Deficiency Judgment: No need to panic.
We can help significantly reduce and ultimately eliminate unsecured notes and deficiency judgments.
Promissory Note: A promissory note is also an unsecured note and a con-
tract between the lender and borrower where the borrower agrees
to pay the difference (or a percentage of the difference) between
the amount owed and the sales price of the property. This is usually presented during a short sale and can only be enforced if the borrower agrees in writing. These notes are also negotiable after the
short sale.

Why you are better off pursuing a short sale vs. a foreclosure.

In Washington State, a majority of foreclosures will be non-judicial,
meaning that the lender will not be able to pursue you, the borrower, for a deficiency judgment. However, in other states, as well
as some WA based lenders, do proceed with judicial foreclosures
and borrowers may be liable to pay a deficiency judgment.

The number one reason to be an advocate pursuing a short sale vs.
a foreclosure, is that a foreclosure (regardless of whether it is a non-
judicial or judicial foreclosure), will prevent you from obtaining a
mortgage for a minimum of 5 years, in addition to extensive damage to your credit, whereas a short sale will have far less damage
to your credit in that most borrowers will be able to obtain a mortgage after 2 years of conducting a short sale. Also, the deficiency
(or tax consequences) in the event of foreclosure, if is collectable,

will be significantly higher than in a short sale (since properties sell at extremely discounted prices at foreclosure auctions).

The second reason why we advocate short sales is that promissory notes and deficiency judgments before and after the sale are, for the most part, **negotiable. In many cases, the deficiency owed can be negotiated to a percentage (i.e. 10% of a HELOC loan) or sometimes completely waived.** The lender may forgive the balance in exchange for a small pay off or an affordable payment arrangement with the borrower. This largely depends on two factors:

- The strength of the negotiator
- Lender policy and type of loan. *Sometimes, it is even possible to have the buyer pay the difference!

Again, should the lender reserve the right to pursue a deficiency, at least you have a short sale on your credit report vs. a foreclosure. Keep in mind that it is rare for the lender to actually pursue the deficiency and therefore the unsecured note will most likely be replaced with a 1099 issued by the IRS for the taxes owed on the sale. You will want to explore the Mortgage Forgiveness Debt Relief Act of 2007 to verify whether you are exempt from this tax.

In addition, if the lender pursues the remaining deficiency, the deficient amount can, even after the short sale, be negotiated down further. Keep in mind, there are situations where the lender will absolutely not allow a short sale unless the homeowner signs a promissory note for the full amount of the difference. In these situations, a professional short sale negotiator can aggressively negotiate the balance before the short sale as much as possible. Sellers will want to explore these options before considering filing for bankruptcy.

"On a short sale, will I have to pay the bank the difference between what I owe and the final sales price of my property?"

Yes: As we discussed earlier, the lender may ask you to pay the difference in the form of a promissory note and will not allow a short sale unless a note for the full amount is signed by the borrower or the "right to reserve to pursue a deficiency" is outlined in a statement signed by you. In these situations, again, it may be in your best interest to negotiate down the balance as much as possible before the short sale, then negotiate the balance even further after the short sale (if the deficiency is actually pursued by the lender/pmi/collections agency).

No: It is possible, in a short sale, to negotiate the deficiency owed down to a percentage that can be paid or to even waive the liability completely. #That's OUR GOAL! What this means is that, say, if you owe $700K to your lender but your property sells for $550K, a strong negotiator may be able to get the lender to settle at $550K and **not** pursue the deficiency with the homeowner (in exchange for a pay off or sometimes a payment arrangement with the borrower). That means the homeowner will be able to walk away from their short sale (although they may owe the IRS a tax for the difference, which most homeowners are eligible for exemption under the Mortgage Forgiveness Debt Relief Act of 2007). A negotiator will accomplish this by demonstrating to the lender what their losses will be in the event that you, the borrower, allow the property to go into foreclosure or if you file for bankruptcy. The negotiator will argue that it is in their best interest to proceed with the short sale, and will present all the market data, financial comparison sheet, etc. in order to make a strong case.

CHAPTER 7:

Baby Seller On Board!

ONCE YOUR SELLER IS ON-BOARD FOR THE RIDE:
(tell 'em to sit down, shut up, and hold on!) just kidding!

Expectations and Timeline for the Seller
MARKETING YOUR HOME:
- Your home will be shown to both investors and traditional buyers.
- I put a sign as i do in any listing, and have a key box.
- I however, **do not make flyers**, as i like to control the questions to the best of my ability. I like the potential buyers to call me off the sign and or the agents to call me directly with questions. I do this because i can set the groundwork and get a feel for who is serious. I can also control hype if i am getting lots of action.
- **I take very Basic photos**. A far cry from my professional photographer days. (Unless it is a luxury home and i still need to obtain the buyer from the high-end market. But, even then, **i take minimal shots**). I tend to use my iphone, as the photos are great but not awesome and they upload easily to my computer. I take between 5-10 shots. I don't want too many. The reason i do this is because the

eventual appraiser or BPO agent will be looking at these shots also. I need this home to appraise as low as possible for me to get approval on my asking price.

- **I ask that the Sellers not go crazy cleaning and fixing up the home**. Again, we need the house to appraise on the lower end of the spectrum. If the bank comes back with a higher price they will counter our offer and the likelihood of our offer being approved is null and void. #have to be smarter than the average Joe here people! **It's alright if its messy—that's just fine and dandy!**
- **Marketing remarks are BASIC**. Enough to draw a buyer, but not over the top and crazy. Again, the bank, the BPO agent and possibly a lien holder appraiser will be seeing these.
- **The goal is to get the highest and best offer in the shortest time possible**. Those viewing or calling to view the home have been instructed not to bother the seller with questions regarding short sale so as to not put any additional stress on the seller. I put in my remarks to call me with ANY questions regarding the short sale.
- Some Sellers don't want their home advertised as a short sale. I explain that it has to be in the remarks for agents to see. It does not have to be in the remarks for the public to see. With RedFin, it will show up in a Basic search, but for most people searching on the MLS it won't show. *again, the back alley abortion embarrassment.

THE OFFER:
- Once an offer is received on the property, i schedule an appointment for the seller to come in and sign the purchase agreement. Although the seller(s) do need to sign the offer, the property can attract multiple offers (we hope so). All offers will be submitted to the seller (Homeowner) for

review. The best offer will be signed, the others that are there at that time or come in the future, will be put into 1st back up, 2nd back up, accordingly. Agents are kept in the loop throughout the transaction with weekly updates and can call with questions at any time.

- The "seller" who signs the offer is the Home Owner. They still own the home and are agreeing to apply for short sale with their lender. But in the end, after the lender accepts the offer the "seller" becomes the Lender/Lien holder. The Home Owner will sign at escrow to close the transaction, transferring ownership to the new buyer/owner, just like a regular sale.
- If a buyer asks for "Seller paid closing costs", then the "seller" is the bank. That will be part of what is being negotiated and the bottom net number the bank is receiving. The Homeowner will sign the offer, but the bank needs to ok the terms. If it is accepted, the "seller", the Bank, will have accepted the offer amount, less the closing costs and it will be stated in a letter of approval that can be reviewed prior to closing.

THE PROCESS:
- Once we have sent the offer to the Lender(s), the actual short sale process can take anywhere from 4 weeks to 4 months. This timeline varies with each lender.
- Always keep all parties informed at least weekly. Keeping the seller at ease, the buyers on board and excited, and the selling office agent educated on the process will be of utmost importance.
- After each lender reviews the short sale Packaged, a BPO (broker price opinion) will be ordered by the lender. This is similar to an appraisal and once the lender receives their report they will usually make a final decision shortly thereafter.
- The lenders order the BPO/Home Valuation/and in some cases Appraisals so they can figure out what their net proceeds

will be (how much of a loss they will be writing off). The property will remain "Active" or "Pending Back Up" or, "Pending" until the lender(s) accept the offer. **I TRY AND NEGOTIATE THE PROPERTY TO EITHER STAY ACTIVE OR AT THE VERY LEAST GO INTO PENDING BACK UP.** (so on your short sale addendum, make sure you negotiate to keep it active. I find that if i explain to the selling office agent, everyone is on board). I believe it is the best option for my Sellers and i explain to the buyers that all other offers go into back up, so it is not going to hurt them, but acts as a safety net for our effort and hard work in pushing a deal through, in the off chance the buyer drops out.

- Please be patient through this process. At times you may feel things are going too slow, but remember this is not a regular transaction and can take longer to complete. I CONTINUALLY REMIND AGENTS, BUYERS AND SELLERS, of this fact. I always over estimate time frames and if it comes back sooner—everyone is psyched!

THE ACCEPTED OFFER:
- Once an offer has been approved by the lender, i will notify you that we are going to proceed to close the transaction.
- The lender may demand to close escrow anywhere from 10-30 days, so be prepared. If the buyer does not close by the lender's deadline, an extension needs to be applied for and can be timely as well as not guaranteed.
- If the buyer(s) cannot perform and close on time, the lender may decide to proceed with foreclosure thus severing the opportunity for all parties involved to complete a successful transaction.
- Again--- it is important to keep the selling office agent, the buyer(s), escrow, title as well as the buyer(s) loan officer continually updated throughout the process so that when

the bank says "JUMP", you can say "HOW HIGH?" and get it done.

THE CLOSE OF ESCROW:
- You as the Seller, will be instructed to sign seller documents at the escrow office. Please bring with you your ID, all keys, garage door openers, and a good attitude. There will be escrow instructions to follow, like usual.
- It is just like a regular sale, except that the seller will not receive any proceeds from the sale and will be released of the deficiency per the agreement they have made prior with the lien holder(s).
- We will celebrate your new freedom from this financial burden and stress. The monkey off your back will feel pretty awesome!

YOUR FINANCIAL FREEDOM:
- Keep all of your copies of the documents pertaining to this sale in a safe place.
- Try not to incur any new debt and try to keep low balances on any credit cards you may have. Maintain good consumer credit by not paying late on your currently active accounts.
- Pay your rent by check or some other way that can be tracked to show evidence that you are paying on time. This will help you should you choose to purchase a new property in the future.

CHAPTER 8:

Survival Of The Fittest.

BUILD YOUR TEAM--- !

ESCROW

You had BETTER THE HELL partner with the BEST DAMN Escrow officer you know and love. You will come to find that this relationship will keep you either on top of it, or sinking fast.

My escrow relationship is the grease in the wheel of my successful short sale reputation.

It is imperative to be able to forward the offer, set up escrow, and have an estimated HUD1 sent back to me in a timely manner. I prefer same day, but depending on how busy the office is, it can sometimes be the next day.

As SOON as i receive an offer that is in mutual, i forward to escrow—detailing the transaction and request a HUD1 at the earliest convenience. I need the HUD1 to add to my short sale packet and cannot start the process without it.

Throughout the process, i will need to tweak numbers and will need revisions. Those revisions need to be returned to the bank in a timely manner as well.

I cannot stress how important it is to have a well-versed escrow agent/company who understands short sales and understands the need to be on top of it.

TITLE

Title is ALWAYS important. But with short sales they can tell us a lot.

Before i list the home, i have title do a preliminary search for liens that may come up. Mechanical Liens, Construction Liens, or random debts that are lien-ing the property. It is imperative to know what you are dealing with when negotiating a short sale.

If i list a condo that has back HOA dues totaling $2900 that show up as a lien, i need to make sure i am including that on my HUD1 when i present my offer to the bank. If that is forgotten on the HUD1, guess what happens? At closing it will show up and there will be an approval from the bank, that does not include back taxes, HOA dues, or a utility bill and guess who has to pay for that out of their commission? That's right—**not ME**, because i made sure all that was accounted for.

It is not only important that Title be on top of things, but Title and Escrow need to work well together as a team and coupled with a good, smart agent--- will make a success story out of a short sale transaction that could have otherwise gone awry.

REAL ESTATE LAWYER

YOU JUST NEED ONE. Ask around, Google, or research in some other way, but find a local representative--- call around, talk to them on the phone, meet with them. It is important to speak with them and get their view on short sales verses foreclosure. Sometimes Lawyers can be socially retarded and their mannerisms can be annoying *(ok, i was married to one for 10 years so i am a LITTLE bias. **AND** i did birth his offspring, which thankfully are more ME than **HIM**, but i digress)*, just make sure you are in agreement and have similar personalities so when you refer your client to them, you are all speaking the same language. I met with 5 or 6 Lawyers specializing in RE before i related to one professionally. My clients appreciate the referral, the Lawyer appreciates the referral and we work together as a team, verses me accidentally sending my clients into a wolf den. You don't want a lawyer who doesn't have a full grasp of short sales (there are some out there that think they are God) and will potentially freak out your client. Find one that understands and explains in stressed-out homeowner speak. Lawyer speak is **SCARY** for everyone.

REAL ESTATE ACCOUNTANT/CPA

Again, you JUST NEED ONE. You aren't a freaking accountant, even if you WERE a math major and do all your own bookkeeping. (ok that's me).... Anyway, laws are changing, and with foreclosures and short sales on the rise there are constant changes happening in the tax world. There is no way in hell you will stay on top of it. So--- find your accountant soul mate (if that's possible) and refer away. Mine is a lifesaver--- he explains things incredibly well without freaking out the client. They don't leave concerned that the IRS is after them. He explains the tax liabilities and gets the usual freak out, nervous break down that typically happens, under control.

CHAPTER 9:

The Vault.

THE VAULT. <------- That's ME. *(...and Bentley, my hairy cohort)*

WHAT I NEED FROM MY "MOTIVATED" SELLERS
Ok. This is what i mean about needing to make sure your seller(s) are motivated. While i am preparing a Listing Agreement, **i need to get a TON of their personal information, not intended but usually feeling like i am asking for their first born child, their DNA and of course their full trust in confidentiality and safe record keeping.** It's a lot to expect someone to just hand over. And most people aren't all that organized, especially when they are in the middle of chaos. So it's good to get everything ahead of time to ease the pain for everyone involved.

SOoo *(i do that a lot. I like to really Express the way i am saying words, SOooooo and draw it out, bc its funny.)*

SOooo..... the Sellers are on board, i have qualified them as good candidates and we have explained all the nuances of short sales. They may have spoken with a lawyer or an accountant and feel that this is the best decision for them. I have given them a market analysis and we know what our goal range is.

When I need to get some info, I email them this:

Dear

  Jack and Jill, (the goody two-shoes couple that don't want the neighbors to know),

  Bert and Ernie, (the relatively normal couple, although currently separated)

  Bonnie and Clyde, (have moved out, taken the range, the fridge, and all the light fixtures)

  Helen Keller, (taken advantage of because she couldn't see what she was signing with the loan officer)

  Frat Boy and Sorority Girl, (spent their HELOC on 2 new cars, a boob job, and a trip to Australia)

  Daisy (moved to an intentional community--- smokin' copious amounts of pot. Living on unemployment)

  Thelma & Louise (left on a road trip, call if you get a buyer, we'll try and find a fax machine)

Or **Heather and Craig** (Happily married, will get through anything, God Bless)

Below is the information I need to short sale your property.... The worse the situation is, the better for me to negotiate. So be honest, and please don't be embarrassed. My job is to get the monkey off your back. As soon as I receive the info, i can prepare paperwork and get a game plan. It will give me a good idea of how to proceed with this individual property and we can have a more thorough and successful transaction. Selling/negotiating a short sale is nothing like listing a traditional sale

Please provide information: (please note that i keep this info in the strictest of confidence).

Address of property:_____

Purchase Price _____ **(one or two loans originally/how much each)**

Purchase Year_____

First Mortgage: (name of bank)_____ / $_____   estimate amount owed

Second Mortgage: (name of bank) _____ / $_____   estimate amount owed

Any other liens on property: (i.e.: 3rd mortgage/taxes/utilities/any others?)

HOA dues (how much per month)_____   How   many   months behind?_____

How   much   are   taxes   on   this   property   per   year?   (if   you know)_____

How much do you think the value is, if sold right now _____ Why?_____

How motivated are you to sell?_____

What is your hardship/reason to sell?_____
_____

Have   you   or   are   you   planning   on   filing bankruptcy?_____

Have   you   ever   applied   for   a   loan   modification?_____   What   was the outcome?_____

Social Security #'s of each person on title_____
_____

That should get us up and running and will allow me to prepare to contact your individual bank(s) and see if this is a workable solution for you.

Please feel free to discuss anything at anytime. I am always available by phone or email.

After I receive this information I will couple it with our market / price calculation, based on the short sale process. Per our earlier conversation, the listing price will target a quick sale, and will be <u>estimated </u>around a price point that will be within an agreeable range for the bank. My goal is to calculate a number that is more profitable for the bank to short sale versus foreclose. The price will be low enough to generate fast interest from the public (hopefully) and yet the bank will be agreeable.

There will be specific paperwork your bank needs you to fill out. I will be forwarding all required documents and request what is needed as soon as I contact your banks specifically.

I look forward to hearing from you.

CHAPTER 10:

Record Keeping

Get that organizational cap on and keep it there!

I keep a record of each bank i have worked with. So i have a LIST of phone numbers, fax numbers, email contacts i have worked with, as well as notes on what is needed for a short sale packet to be submitted.

If i haven't worked with a certain bank, i look them up online, or call directly to find out what is needed to submit a short sale.

What i have found is that all Banks are pretty similar, so i have made my own system and request the following from my clients via email:

Hello!

<u>Attached</u> are a few simple forms i will need to negotiate with the bank:

- **an authorization to speak with me,**
- **a financial statement describing where money is going**
- **an explanation of hardship**

In addition, i will need the following documents as soon as possible:

- Please draft a hardship letter. I have provided an example of wording in the attached documents.
- The bank requires proof of income i.e.: 60 days of pay stubs, or a profit and loss statement over the past 60 days,
- Last three months bank statements,
- Last 2 years tax returns
- as well as the financial sheet i have attached

Since this is a book and not a computer, (duh), I cannot attach the forms I use. However I can give you the jist.
In addition, you can always download the information or request it to be faxed to you directly from the bank(s) you are dealing with for that particular transaction.

The Authorization. You need this to speak with the banks on the clients' behalf.
You can use the banks forms, or use your own.
I have created my own--- and use it over and over again.

BANK AND FINANCIAL INSTITUTION AUTHORIZATION AND RELEASE FORM

I hereby authorize (agent's name), (name of real estate company) and (escrow/closing officer), (name of Escrow Company/Closing Agency), to request, obtain and verify any and all mortgage loan information, including but not limited to, payoff, arrearage, and reinstatement amounts as well as financial history. The information obtained is to be used for the purpose of facilitating the resolution of my foreclosure.

Property Address:_____

Loan Number_____

Loan Number _____

Borrower Signature_____

_____

Print Name   Date

Social Security Number:_____

Date of Birth:_____

_____

_____

Co-Borrower Signature_____

_____

Print Name   Date

Social Security Number: _____

Date of Birth:_____

Financial Statement

You will need to download the financial statement needed from a bank, or individually from each bank you are working with. It is part of the short sale packet required for each transaction. I have just used one of them for years as it is basic and they are all generally the same.

The bank needs to know how much money is coming in and how much is going out and how much the seller has to verify why they cannot afford their home.

Sorry. I don't feel like typing out the financial statement for you right now. I'd have to use excel and everything. #that's a lot of unnecessary work. Excel is not my friend.

So don't be lazy ~~like me~~, just go to the bank website, any bank website, and download a short sale packet. You can use the same financial statement over and over. Just keep it in your file- scan it, and save it on email. **I keep everything I need on pdf and just shoot it off when I need to.** It saves a lot of time that way.

Hardship Letter Guidelines

Hardships: What are your current hardships (current and past)? For example: unemployed, car accident, medical problems (personal or family), etc. Go into a little detail about each hardship. The following are the most important messages to get across to the Lender:

- Why you will not be able to be current again on your loan.
- We do not have enough income to make these payments
- We are leaving the property
- We have been turned down for a loan modification

Your Assets- Explain that you have no assets with which to continue paying

Bankruptcy- You could also mention "I don't want to have to file bankruptcy".

\<Sample Hardship Letter>

To Whom It May Concern:

I have been unable to make my payments on my house, and I am now facing foreclosure. My inability to keep up with the monthly payments is the result of (loss of job, illness, accident, death or disability of a wage earner- describe in detail what the hardship is).

In spite of my current financial difficulties, I expect that it will only get worse. I am not in a position to continue making my mortgage payments. This was not at all what I intended but I have come to the conclusion that this is my only option.

I am doing what I can to not be forced to file bankruptcy and include the home.

Your help and consideration in this matter are very much appreciated.

Signature
Printed Name
Date

CHAPTER 11:

Love Letters. #swoon.

Let's talk HARDSHIP. Hardship Letters to be exact. I just HEART Hardship letters.

I call them LOVE letters, because i LOVE to see what people are going to write about for their hardship LETTERS! #BahaHAha-haHA! And boy have i seen some doozies! **#no judgment.**

SO LET'S DO A CHAPTER ON HARDSHIP's ALL ON IT's OWN. It's worth it.

I have taken out names, but would like to show you a few i have received as a plea to the banks for help and assistance.

No shit. <u>These are seriously letters i have received.</u>
No. I didn't submit them. I had to suggest some, um, modifications…

Letter 1:

Please Help Me. No one else will.

My life has become a depressing country western song. Sad but true.

I lost my job, and my husband left me, the bastard. He said i wasn't his sugar momma any more so he left and never came back. He left me with all 5 children and 2 of them aren't even mine, they were his other two skanks kids and i can't even track them down.

I am selling the tires off my car to get groceries this week, and the kids are hitchhiking (it's not that far) to school, but its ok because some of the neighbors feel badly for us so they are giving them rides. The church has donated clothes and i have been forced to borrow my 12 year olds paper route money to keep the heat on. He's a pretty good saver.

I have credit card debt (4 cards) and a car payment even though the car will not have tires and i can't afford to pay that either.

I am considering selling my wedding ring but i have to lose some weight first because i can't get it off.

I cannot make the payments on my house. Please consider me as a candidate for your short sale program. I want to file bankruptcy but i can't afford to hire the lawyer.

Sincerely,

Letter 2:

To Whom It May Concern:

I am self employed and i haven't been very responsible i guess. I thought i had enough for the rainy day fund but its only been 6 months and my fund is gone. I tried to modify the loans, i have 2 and am behind on taxes, but you guys won't work with me.

I am a massage therapist and i don't have any clients. They just quit calling. I am depressed. My wife and i are fighting and i think we are headed toward a divorce. Luckily we don't have any kids. She is trying to get a job at Starbucks because they have benefits after 90 days and she says as soon as she gets a couple of paychecks she is leaving me.

I can't make my mortgage payment any longer. You will see what i am talking about when you see my profit and loss statement.

I know i sound depressed but i don't know what else to do. Please help.

Sincerely,

Letter 3:

To Whom It May Concern:
I have been unable to make my payments on my house, i am now facing foreclosure. My inability to keep up with my payments is a result of a profound spiritual awakening I had 2 years ago. I have now quit my job and am living at as an artist in an intentional community. I have no income.

In spite of my current financial difficulties, i expect that things will only get better. I have realized that joy, love, passion, and purpose it far more important than my credit score and status in the corporate world. Unfortunately, i am not in a position to continue making my mortgage payments. This is not at all what i intended but i have come to the conclusion that this is my only option.

Your help and consideration in this matter are very much appreciated.

Letter 4:

DEAR BANK WHO RUINED MY LIFE:

I BOUGHT MY DREAM HOUSE ON A GREAT LOAN THAT I COULD AFFORD IN 2006.
I CANT AFFORD IT NOW.

I WAS JUST LAYED OFF 2 MONTHS AGO OFF AFTER 14 YEARS WITH MY COMPANY AND WITH MY LOAN ADJUSTMENTS NOW

COMING MONTHLY I CAN'T KEEP UP. WE COULDNT' KEEP UP BEFORE I WAS LAYED OFF.

MY WIFE AND I ARE SO STRESSED OUT WE GO OUT SAILING EVERY DAY TO TRY AND NOT HAVE A NERVOUS BREAKDOWN. LUCKILY THAT IS FREE FOR US AS OUR HOME IS ON THE WATER. WE DONT WANT THE HOUSE TO GO INTO FORECLOSURE BECAUSE IT WOULD BE EMBARRASSING IF THE NEIGHBORS FOUND OUT.

WE HAVE CUT BACK A LOT ALREADY. WE SOLD OUR 3RD AND 4TH CARS AND ARE NOT GOING TO OUR LAKE HOUSE THIS YEAR.

I MAY HAVE A NEW JOB BUT IT WILL BE AT A MUCH REDUCED SALARY. I AM NOT SURE I WILL TAKE IT AS WE ARE SO CONCERNED ABOUT WHAT IS HAPPENING WITH OUR HOME THAT I DON'T THINK I CAN WORK RIGHT NOW.
MY WIFE HAS NOT HAD TO WORK AND WON'T.

WE HAVE BEEN TOLD THAT IF WE SHORT SALE THE HOME IT WILL NOT BE AS BAD AS A FORECLOSURE ON OUR RECORD.

WE ARE SORRY WE HAVE NOT PAID FOR THE PAST 17 MONTHS. WE HAVE BEEN VERY STRESSED OUT.

WE WOULD LIKE PERMISSION TO TAKE THE WOLFE RANGE AND THE SUB ZERO WITH US WHEN WE MOVE.

THANK YOU FOR YOUR HELP.

YOURS TRULY,

Letter 5:

My wife and I have outgrown our home. We tried for a loan modification but were turned down. We were told to short sale. We took our home equity line of credit, bought a new car, and a new house. We cannot afford to keep both houses. We have tried to sell the house for almost a year with no success so now we are forced to lower the price which puts us in short sale status. We are not wanting to cash out our 401K or touch any of our investment accounts. If you don't short sale we will simply hand the keys back as we don't want the house anymore. We have taken the appliances, all the light fixtures, door knobs and anything of value we feel we put into the home.
If it goes to foreclosure, we will come back and take the carpet and potentially the hardwoods.

Thank you for your consideration.

Oh, i have more. <you got a good chuckle, though, didn't you?> but it's really not nice for me to laugh at these.
Honestly--- everyone has their problems and they are not very comical until you see how seriously comical it is when reading a hardship letter.

That being said, the above letters were not used in that form and the Sellers, with a little advice, tweaked them.
Each of these clients successfully sold their home in a short sale. Believe it or not.

*In the end of this sometimes, comical, process, I have to make mention that there really are people in tough situations. If you have been watching the news, I am sure you are aware of the job layoffs, and understand the economical place our country is truly in. Families are trying to survive without filing bankruptcy and without losing absolutely everything they have. Throw a divorce or health issue into the cycle and it's becoming an ever increasingly familiar situation. Not all hardship letters are funny. In fact, most aren't. Just remember **the goal of a hardship letter is to CONVINCE the mortgage company(s) that the homeowner's financial hardship is so horrible that they cannot correct the situation without assistance from the lender.**

CHAPTER 12:

So, Now Where Are We?

We have identified it will be a short sale listing, explained to the seller the pro's and con's and referred any legal and tax advice questions to a professional. They have decided to move forward. You have given them a list of paperwork to provide you as well as financials and personal information and their first-born child.

You have a target range for an offer and are listing the home.

I do not list the home until I have all the financial information, authorization, etc. so that I am ready to go as soon as I receive an offer.

Now I have received an offer—and we are in mutual.

My example listing was listed at $320K. I received an offer after 1 week on the market for $315K with $5000 in seller paid closing costs. The seller has 2 lien holders, the same bank in this situation.

WHAT DO I DO?

Even though both the lien holders are the same bank, they are handled separately.

I call both departments. The first lien holder has a phone number and fax number and short sale packet needed to set up with loss mitigation (short sale department). And the second lien holder (HELOC in this situation) has its own phone number, fax number and short sale packet needed to set up with their loss mitigation department.

I immediately set up escrow.

I email the offer with the purchase price, the buyer(s) names, the seller(s) names, and the loan officer contact info for the buyer, as well as the title company contact info. I also spell out both agent's names and their firms. I give contact info for everyone involved (email and phone).

I let escrow know that this file has 2 loans (my example) The purchase price is $315K with $5K in seller paid closing costs.

The first loan is estimated to be $420K and the second is $50K. That's right, I am selling a house for $315K that the seller owes $470K on. It's not uncommon.

When there is a second lien holder I direct escrow to put 10% of the unpaid balance toward the second on the HUD1. I also ask that escrow check with title and verify that all liens are included. If that information is not readily accessible we estimate high on everything. Over estimate--- you don't want to go back and have to add to the net loss for the bank. My example listing is a house, not a condo so we don't have any back HOA dues and taxes are current.

Here is a trick I use: <u>I ask for **2 HUD's** from escrow</u>.

- The first one I give 10% of the unpaid balance to the second and I submit that one with the short sale packet to the first lien holder.
- The second HUD I ask for only $1K to be given to the second lien holder. I use this HUD to submit my short sale packet to my second lien holder.

That way--- *this is brilliant*--- the first sees a larger amount and may jones us down to a smaller amount. The second is going to see a smaller amount and tell us their bottom dollar amount needed, what they HAVE to have. So--- part of the negotiation is done. Then, once I receive approval from the first and know the most I can give the second--- I will hopefully have prepped the second and they will be happy with what they receive. #of course this is in a perfect world.

Once I receive the estimated HUD1 from escrow I can move forward and submit my short sale packet(s).
I put together my already received seller information in the order it is requested by each loss mitigation department.
Generally a Short Sale packet includes this: (they are all different, so verify each time) and MAKE SURE EVERYTHING IS IN THE PACKET WHEN YOU SEND IT. If the packet is not complete, the bank will ignore you. Check, Double Check and Check again... or it's a waste of your time, your clients time and the buyers time.

1) **Authorization**
2) **Hardship Letter**
3) **Financial Statement**
4) **Copies of last 2 months pay stubs or profit and loss statement**
5) **Copies of last 2 months bank statements**
6) **Copies of last 2 years tax returns**
7) **Offer**
8) **Buyers pre-approval letter**
9) **Estimated HUD1**
10) **Listing Agreement**
11) **List of any repairs needed on the property (to help depreciate)**
12) **I also include my CMA , whether they ask for it or not**

- I put the loan number on each page in the same corner (Adobe has a great program for this) (I used to hire my daughter to write it in the corner).
- I then fax it to the loss mitigation department to set up the file. **I use efax—because it's AWESOME.** I can scan the (usual 200 page file) to myself and then save as a pdf. Go onto efax and upload it and voila! I fax it--- it's received and I get an email once it has been received.
- Much more easy breezy than standing at a fax machine re-faxing over and over again, a shit load of pages, with the busy bank fax machines that require patience and getting up at 3:00 am to get the fax to actually go through. I'm not kidding. Believe me. You will pull your freaking hair out.
- Get an efax. It will save your sanity.

Once the **COMPLETE SHORT SALE** file is successfully faxed. (Please make sure the complete short sale package was faxed. It is a huge waste of everyone's time as it will delay the short sale set up, if it is not complete. Do it right the first time. Send it in one, complete package and verify receipt.).I call within 24 hours to make sure it was received and uploaded into the system. The bank will look for your authorization, and ask you the loan number, the last four digits of the seller(s) social security number, the address etc, to verify you are authorized. So be prepared. File in front of you.

I always ask the bank for their individual timeline/timeframe and what to expect.

Once the short sale is uploaded into the system a BPO is ordered. Remember that word? BPO is a **b**roker's **p**rice **o**pinion. The bank hires ~~some jackass~~ an agent to valuate the property and tell them what the current market value is. But remember, the banks are located all over the US. Most are not local to your listing. So, they call a database of agents that work in a certain zip code and I swear seem to always be out of area agents, and that lucky duck calls you for access to the house. So, they generally don't know the neighborhood at all, zero, zilch! And it is your job to educate them.

Another important trick: take the lockbox off the door. And drop the price to at or just slightly above your offer price on the MLS. While you are waiting for your BPO to happen, it is more important that you control the outcome to the best of your ability, then anything else, so take the lockbox off the house so that you will have to meet the agent at the house and allow access. I have my CMA with comps already printed out, I point out the flaws in the house, I call my clients and say, don't make the beds tomorrow--- and hopefully they will get the hint and leave dirty dishes out, --- get my drift?
Your BPO agent is going to pull your listing information to compare and shop for comps.
So, control access, have information readily available to help the BPO agent, and make sure the listing is priced near your offer. **Whatever value this BPO agent comes back with will be your death or your glory.** It will be another 6 months before you can demand another BPO. I have argued BPO's before, even hired appraisals. I have only won 2 times. It is VERY difficult to argue the value that comes back from a BPO.

~~Even if they are stupid heads dummies that don't even know the area~~

So, befriend that agent, try and get their email or phone number and do your best to get he or she on your side. Follow up with them, and thank them! #nuff said.

Once the BPO is turned into the bank—usually about 10 days. I follow up daily with the bank until I am assigned to a negotiator.
LOG ALL COMMUNICATIONS. NAME, CONTACT INFO, DATE. Always.
I bug, I request the file to be expedited and I do what I can to sugar the hell out of the situation until I am assigned a name. Once I get

the name I ask for phone numbers, extensions and emails. I follow up in every way possible. It can take 2-4 weeks for the bank to complete valuations and then you will either be approved or countered.

Remember: You can always counter. And you can counter again.
It's all about negotiations. (but, that's another book).
After countering is done, submission for approval can take anywhere from 24 hours to 10 business days, depending on the bank.

ALWAYS keep your buyers, Sellers, and selling office agent abreast throughout the process. It is important to keep them holding on and eager to move forward. Buyers and selling office agents often walk away if they feel things are not progressing.

Once you have approval form the first, if you only have a seller with one lien then **OH YA BABY**, you are done and ready to proceed to close per the approval letter received just like a normal, non short sale transaction.

If you have a second lien, (like my example), then we forward the approval letter and approved HUD1 to the second and let them know what the terms are.
The process is the same as above for the first lien holder.

Once you have received approval from both lien holders, then **OH DOUBLE YA BABY**, you are done and ready to proceed to close per the approval letter(s) received, just like a normal, non short sale transaction! And if you've done a good job, the buyer is still there, excited for the deal they are getting and the loan officer is ready to rock and roll and life is good!

CHAPTER 13:

This Chapter Has Two Names (I just couldn't decide)

LEAVE ME ALONE, YOU BASTARDS!
DON'T ANSWER THE PHONE IF IT'S A 1- 800 OR 1-877 NUMBER CALLING!

Sometimes I get a seller that's a real worrywart and is having a literal nervous breakdown about the lender repeatedly calling ~~imagine that~~ because they have missed payments on their home.

INSTEAD OF SAYING, **"WHAT IN THE HELL DID YOU THINK WAS GOING TO HAPPEN IF YOU QUIT MAKING YOUR EFFING PAYMENTS?"** OR **GET A GRIP! JUST DON'T ANSWER THE FREAKIN PHONE...** OR **JESUS, MARY AND JOSEPH!** OR, **REALLY? WHY ARE YOU CALLING ME? I AM NOT THE ONE WHO MISSED 14 MORTGAGE PAYMENTS!?**

I send them a **No Contact** letter to A) help appease freaked out seller and B) to hopefully help lessen or stop the calls.

Of course this is not a 100% guarantee, but most banks will abide by the following letter.

PLEASE DO NOT CONTACT ME BY PHONE

First Loan #_____   Second Loan #_____

First Lender: _____   Second Lender: _____

Property Address: _____

According to the Fair Lending Law, I have the right to request that you, my lender, not contact me by phone regarding my loan being in default. I do not wish to speak to any collection agents about this account. Please make any future communication with me in writing or if you must speak to someone regarding this account, please talk to my Real Estate Agent with (company name) (agents name) who is assisting me in selling my home. The information obtained by my agent is to be used for the purpose of facilitating the resolution of my foreclosure.

_____

Borrower
Printed Name _____
Date:_____

Social Security Number: _____
Date of Birth: _____

There is not much we can do about the phone calls and they do get aggressive. Usually this helps.

Once a property has an offer and is in "short sale" status, the phone calls **should** stop, as well as any foreclosure proceedings. It is rare the foreclosure date will not be staved off until the short sale is finalized. But always check to make sure. Ask the bank if there is a foreclosure date set? If there is one, verify that they are holding off until after the short sale has been negotiated.

CHAPTER 14:

The Many Hats

So there you have it. My example listing is closed. The sellers are relieved, the Buyers are psyched. I made some moo-lah. In the end it's about helping homeowners with a positive alternative to going to foreclosure. It feels good to help out in a situation like this.

I have realized I am not just a real estate agent.
I am much more.

When dealing with short sales, the truth is, you wear a lot of hats AND they aren't all pretty ones:

Realtor (selling the dream, or at least it WAS their dream at one time)
Guesstimator, Appraiser, BPO estimator, (estimating where banks going to value the property)
Marriage Counselor/Therapist (dealing with stressed clients/couples)
Marketing Specialist (selling quickly with short sale finesse)
Negotiator, (patient, dubious, forthright, and befriending the devil.)
Enemy/Friend (clients are like Jekyll and Hyde / and so are the banks)
Rock To Lean On (clients need someone to assure them, sympathize and understand)
Target To Abuse (clients need someone to abuse, it's your fault they are under water.

Selling Agent Educator (keeping the dipshit selling agents informed) (don't be one of them)

Glue-That-Holds-The-Parts-In-Tact (keeping the buyers on board, and the sellers motivated, the bank interested and greasing the wheel on a continual basis)

Professional Organizer (either YOU are, you figure out how to be, or you HIRE one)

Master Faxer (e.fax is your best friend. You will only use the old school fax once and you will agree)

Phone Annoyer (paid to bug, harass and get your way)

Multi-Tasker (circus juggler/hat model)

Chocolate Lover and Coffee Drinker (you will need the pick me up and the hOo hA to keep going)

But DON'T let the latter lead to

Fat Ass. (easy to do when sucking down lattes at a desk all day, especially if those latte's are mocha's) #not that I would know anything about that

Wear your hats well!
(I wear my **FAT Ass** one to the gym each day...)

Closing a short sale transaction gives me a high, it makes me feel good that I made a difference and at the end of the day--- which brings me full circle, (right after my fat ass comment) back to gym terminology. Everyone likes to win, don't they?

Now go out there and **GET SOME!**

GRATITUDE.

I was just going to send this book off to the press, when I decided to add this one last bit*...oh, and I also realized my spellcheck had been done in Spanish.*

ON a serious note:

Even though I have been successful at listing, negotiating, and closing short sales, I still have those days when I think "wouldn't it be nice to have a corporate job with benefits, more 9-5 hours, and weekends off, vacation days and a consistent paycheck to count on?"

Sometimes, I just don't know why I keep working so hard, wearing all my hats needed to be successful at this game.

Just last December I had 7 short sale transactions fall apart, right before Christmas. I was incredibly stressed, to say the least. Not only was it a personal financial hit, as I then didn't have funds estimated for the holidays, and for bills, etc. (7 CLOSINGS WORTH!) but, it was coupled with stressed out sellers who were an even more emotional disaster. Each of them sucked me dry calling me, texting me, emailing me multiple times a day, freaking out, and melting down. I was begging for extensions, hollering at buyer's lenders, and trying to organize constant chaos. In the end, 6 of the 7 houses still closed (albeit, later than scheduled and after the holidays). I had to work much harder for those deals, and it felt thankless. it certainly was an emotional rollercoaster while riding through it and I wasn't sure it was worth it. Each night when I came home, my husband read the stress all over me, as it was obviously taking its toll on me. I ended up with pneumonia. Through the holidays and into the New Year I worked from bed with high fevers and absolutely no energy in any part of my being. I didn't want to let my seller(s) down. They may or may not have noticed how sick I really was. All they cared about was how the deal was going. Was it progressing? And how was I going to fix everything?

I find that my short sale sellers seem to feel like they are the ONLY ones I am working with at that time. They call me multiple times a day while their lives are falling apart. I play marriage therapist, listing agent, and short sale negotiator (at a minimum) simultaneously. YES I COULD HAVE BETTER BOUNDARIES, but I am the type of person that feels for everyone and even though I try and leave work AT WORK, I am disastrous at it. From my clients perspective, no one is patient when their life is falling apart o I understand the anxiety that builds. I tend to come home each day feeling the pain from each of my sellers and boy... does it add up sometimes. I start my morning at 6:00 am—answering emails and making east coast phone calls. I never leave my phone throughout the day as a bank could be calling and I don't want to miss it. I deal with sellers, buyers, agents, banks, escrow, title, lawyers, back up offers, all day long. I have to be ON, all day, every day, 7 days a week. I don't imagine a seller will ever know how hard we really work for them, especially on short sales. I am the type of person that internalizes each clients issues and I take them on myself like they are mine. Each deal is imperative to close. Each one is a personal hit if it doesn't. I feel for my sellers and I carry it all on my shoulders until I get the deal done. Well, this last December, I had 3 of my most high maintenance sellers I have ever had, at the same time--- LOTS going on, extensions to be begged for and buyers backing out. I was exhausted. My job felt thankless. I considered leaving real estate. NO. REALLY.

Sometimes, I wonder, --- is it really worth it?

YES, IT IS.
One of my sellers invited me over last night. We toasted, post-close, and to short sale success. Their gratitude was amazing.
They gave me a card that read:
One great, strong, unselfish soul in every community could actually redeem the world. – Elbert Hubbard.
They wrote inside:
Thank you, so very much Joey! Thank you for making a difference.

You transformed our lives in such a wonderful way.

We didn't even realize what a huge energy drain and emotional weight the old house was and thanks to you, we can breathe again. We will always work with you and con-

tinually refer you as the "Best Agent in the World!" We will forever treasure our relationship with you. Thank you from the bottom of our hearts.

Wow. I came home and cried.

I don't know what it was about this card in particular, as I have received several over the years, but it touched me deeply. May be it came at a time when I need to feel thanked. Maybe it is because it was one of the 7 deals I had that horrible month. Maybe because our job is thankless sometimes. Most of the time. Maybe because what was written was how I feel too, and they pegged it.
I have received multiple cards, bottles of champagne, wine, lovely dinners with clients, flowers and other thoughtful gifts over the years, but this one, THIS ONE, felt very special and I happily had a moment of realization that **YES. IT IS WORTH IT.**

Because,
Where would any of us be without our friends, family and those that stand beside us? –Kobi Yamada

That is why I go to work each day, and why I put on the particular hat that I need to wear, and why I push through to get it done. **Because I am the advocate for my clients. I am the one that stands behind them.** it feels wonderful to know I CAN and DO make a difference in someones life.

Being a Realtor, RULES.

SOoo, Who is this, ~~"Joey McCune Moore"~~ self-proclaimed $\mathcal{DIVA}$?

She's a short chick with a BIG personality.

Italian, Catholic, and lover of anything bad-for-you, ALL red wine, sparkles, and the color PINK.

She's a mother, wife, friend, "athlete" {shut up}, realtor, author, and one HELL of a kick ass, short sale minx. Her ~~poor~~ lucky husband often observes, **"Oh Gawd, WHAT IS SHE UP TO NOW?"**

Life with this girl is kind of manic and includes a lot of yelling and hand flailing and inevitably ends in some sort of drama at the end of the day.

A self-described, thirty-nine forever, urban mother of two, very intelligent and quite good looking teens, married to an ::uber hot:: contractor. She's lived in the Pacific Northwest her entire life and proclaims she "will get-the-hell outta-here someday, head for the sun, and never look back".

As a huge animal lover she shares her heart with a "little" dog with a rather "big" attitude. Bentley is of the Cuban descent, loves to dance, will do anything for chicken, is an epileptic, and gets car sick. Resembling a hairy gremlin, he's cute enough to stay around even though he still poops in the house at the age of 3.

She's a Realtor ~~to the stars~~, at TILA Real Estate www.JoeyMcCune.com , www.TILArealestate.com , and a nice girl, the kind of girl you always wanted to know. She also co-owns with-the-hubby, two Construction related companies www.SawhorseDesignBuildofSeattle.com and www.ModernConcreteDesign.com as well as an online sex toy, e.commerce site www.GoBackToBed.com #busy girl.

Short Sale $\mathcal{DIVA}$ was born after a third glass of wine and a long day of hard negotiating. Hubby lovingly referred to her as the SS DIVA because of her love-of-the-drama-ride on the short sale rollercoaster. Now insert uncorking of nearest bottle of wine for glass number 4... *sip.

Voila! She suddenly had an epiphany to author Short Sale $\mathcal{DIVA}$, where she could vent and share insights to managing a short sale while #keepin' it real.

Who doesn't love a nice Italian girl---anyway?

Oh, and by the way --- **she's successfully closed a hell of a lot of short sales.**

www.ingramcontent.com/pod-product-compliance
Lightning Source LLC
Chambersburg PA
CBHW022132170526
45157CB00004B/1848